Quotations FOR A Man's Soul

Compiled by
MICHAEL MAGGIO

PRENTICE HALL PRESS

We're souls having a human experience.

Brian Weiss

TO DAD

vocabulary to identify God, but it's all we have to work with unless we choose non-verbal communication. I believe that our words both form and reflect our values. Referring to God as masculine excludes women from the realm of godhood; as men, we don't want to exclude women from our lives, yet a diminution of them in any sphere is a diminution of us. Rather than changing the language of these quotes to reflect this point, I would simply ask myself and all men to be vigilant in honoring the equality of women in spiritual matters.

Second, and in seeming contradiction to what I have just said, this book contains quotes exclusively by men. Why? Men grow and develop in many contexts, sometimes just with one woman, sometimes just with a child, sometimes just in mixed gender groups, and sometimes just with men. It is here that this book fits in. Occasionally, men have found it easier to deepen our soul work and to heal spiritual and emotional wounds in the company of other men. Such healing and growth invariably enriches our relationships not only with other men but with the entire human family. Since there are virtually no other books of spiritual quotations exclusively by and for men, this book offers another alternative to the ways available to men for enriching our spiritual lives.

Finally, this book is dedicated to my father, who has walked his spiritual talk for 84 years. I have had the gift of his example throughout my life, and he is reflected in every page of this book.

THE PATH

The spiritual path is one of falling on your face, getting up, brushing yourself off, turning and looking sheepishly at God and then taking the next step.

Aurobindo

If one wants to enter a spiritual path, to explore soul, a certain warrior quality is needed. I'm not speaking of defeating someone, but of having a courageous heart.

Jack Kornfield

The first step is what counts: First beginnings are hardest to make and as small and inconspicuous as they are potent in influence, but once they are made, it is easy to add the rest.

Aristotle

Every man's religion is good. There is none of it bad. We are all trying to arrive at the same place according to our own conscience and teachings. It don't matter which road you take.

Will Rogers

Each of us must make our own true way, and when we do, that way will express the universal way.

D.T. Suzuki

If you do not know the way, seek where His footprints are.

Rumi

To the best of my ability, usually under extreme duress, I tried to say yes when God spoke at key points along the path.

Bill McCartney

If you can find a path with no obstacles, it probably doesn't lead anywhere.

Frank Clark

All rising to a great place is by a winding stair.

Francis Bacon

The only way round is through.

Robert Frost

The next message you need is always right where you are.

Ram Dass

What a long journey! What a lot of trouble! Especially considering that I was there all the time.

Kuleki

The longest journey is the journey inward.

Dag Hammarskjöld

And how, you ask, are we to walk the spiritual path? We answer: say little, and love much; give all; judge no man; aspire to all that is pure and good.

White Eagle

The person who tries to stand still on the path will find that it has vanished.

Robert R. Leichtman and Carl Japikse

The song that I came to sing remains unsung
   to this day.
I have spent my days stringing and unstringing
   my instrument.

Rabindranath Tagore

God calls all of you to take the path of the inner truth—and that means taking responsibility for everything that's in you: for what pleases you and for what you're ashamed of, for the rich person inside you and for the poor one. Francis of Assisi called this, "loving the leper within us."

Richard Rohr

You must dare to disassociate yourself from those who would delay your journey. . . . Leave, depart, if not physically, then mentally. Go your own way, quietly, undramatically, and venture toward trueness at last.

Vernon Howard

There is something in every one of you that waits and listens for the sound of the genuine in yourself. It is the only true guide you will ever have. And if you cannot hear it, you will all of your life spend your days on the ends of strings that somebody else pulls.

Howard Thurman

Any path is only a path, and there is no affront, to oneself or to others, in dropping it if that is what your heart tells you.

Carlos Castaneda

I don't want you to follow me or anyone else. I would not lead you into the promised land if I could, because if I could lead you in, somebody else would lead you out.

Eugene V. Debs

No man is great enough or wise enough for any of us to surrender our destiny to. The only way in which anyone can lead us is to restore to us the belief in our own guidance.

Henry Miller

[S tress] is a symptom that you are living somebody else's life, marching to a drumbeat that doesn't syncopate with your personal body rhythms, playing a role you didn't create, living a script written by an alien authority.

Sam Keen

If you expect someone else to guide you, you'll be lost.

James Earl Jones

If they give you lined paper, write the other way. . . .

Juan Ramón Jiménez

What's right with you is the starting point. What's wrong with you is beside the point.

Uranda

Even a slug is a star, if it dares to be its horned and slimy self.

John Hargrave

The last laps of all paths are the same—surrender of the ego.

Ramana Maharshi

Each soul must meet the morning sun, the new sweet earth and the Great Silence alone.

Ohiyesa

You will know more about a person when they tell you who or what they are trying not to be, than you could ever find out from having them speak about who they think they are.

Cliff Barry

Saul owed his conversion neither to true love, nor to true faith, nor to any other truth. It was solely his hatred of the Christians that set him upon the road to Damascus, and to that decisive experience which was to decide the whole course of his life. He was brought to this experience by following with conviction the course in which he was most completely mistaken.

Carl Jung

You've got to be very careful if you don't know where you're going, because you might not get there.

Yogi Berra

The spiritual path is like a Möbius strip, ever returning unto itself, the outer surface becoming the inner surface even as the inner surface is drawing us back to the outer.

Robert R. Leichtman and Carl Japikse

A persistent trap all along the path is pride in one's spiritual purity.

Ram Dass

To find your own way is to follow your own bliss. This involves analysis, watching yourself and seeing where the real deep bliss is—not the quick little excitement, but the real, deep, life-filling bliss.

Joseph Campbell

He liked to go from A to B without inventing the letters between.

John McPhee

Seekers are offered clues all the time from the world of spirit. Ordinary people call these clues coincidences.

Deepak Chopra

All know the way; few actually walk it.

Bodhidharma

Two roads diverged in a wood, and I—I took the one least traveled by, and that has made all the difference.

Robert Frost

You can never step in the same river twice.

Heraclitus

I'll play it first and tell you what it is later.

Miles Davis

THE SACRED IN ALL

God changes his appearance every second.
Blessed is the man who can recognize him in all his disguises.
One moment he is a glass of fresh water, the next your son
bouncing on your knees or an enchanting woman, or perhaps
merely a morning walk.

Nikos Kazantzakis

One of the hardest lessons we have to learn in
this life, and one that many persons never learn, is to see the
divine, the celestial, the pure in the common, the near at
hand—to see that heaven lies about us here in this world.

John Burroughs

To the soul, the ordinary is sacred and the everyday is the primary source of spirituality.

Thomas Moore

As we begin to sense the divine in the "ordinary," our "ordinary" lives will become quite extraordinary.

Richard Carlson

One should hallow all that one does in one's natural life. One eats in holiness, tastes the taste of food in holiness, and the table becomes an altar. One works in holiness, and he raises up the sparks which hide themselves in all tools. One walks in holiness across the fields, and the soft songs of all herbs, which they voice to God, enter into the song of our soul.

Martin Buber

Never take a leaf or move a pebble without asking permission. Always ask permission. That maintains the balance and teaches humility. That leaf you want to pluck could be far more important than the little purpose you have in mind. You don't know—so ask permission first. We can't go on this way, with the modern culture. Plants, species, and animals are dying. We need to listen to the spirits and bring them back.

Don José Matsuwa

If it falls your lot to be a street sweeper, sweep streets as Raphael painted pictures, sweep streets as Michelangelo carved marble, sweep streets as Beethoven composed music, or Shakespeare wrote poetry.

Martin Luther King, Jr.

Work is not always required . . . there is such a thing as sacred idleness, the cultivation of which is now fearfully neglected.

George McDonald

Since human life is sacred, what we have traditionally labeled "secular" is sacred.

Malcolm Boyd

It requires a certain kind of mind to see beauty in a hamburger bun. Yet, is it any more unusual to find grace in the texture and softly curved silhouette of a bun than to reflect lovingly on . . . the arrangement of textures and colors in a butterfly's wing?

Ray Kroc

A machine is as distinctively and brilliantly and expressively human as a violin sonata or a theorem in Euclid.

Gregory Vlastos

If life and the soul are sacred, the human body is sacred.

Walt Whitman

Let the true sacredness of luscious sexuality be
reclaimed.

David Lesser

Every part of this soil is sacred in the estimation
of my people.

Seattle

Every grain of sand has a wonderful soul.

Joan Miró

In music, in the sea, in a flower, in a leaf, in an act
of kindness. . . . I see what people call God in all these things.

Pablo Casals

Everything that God created is potentially holy, and our task as humans is to find that holiness in seemingly unholy situations. When we can do this, we will have learned to nurture our souls.

Harold Kushner

By learning to discover and value our ordinariness, we nurture a friendliness toward ourselves and the world that is the essence of a healthy soul.

Thomas Moore

When humans participate in ceremony, they enter a sacred space. Everything outside of that space shrivels in importance. Time takes on a different dimension. Emotions flow more freely. The bodies of participants become filled with the energy of life, and this energy reaches out and blesses the creation around them. All is made new; everything becomes sacred.

Sun Bear

GRACE

There is nothing but God's grace. We walk upon it; we breathe it; we live and die by it.

Robert L. Stevenson

Grace says you have nothing to give, nothing to earn, nothing to pay.

Charles Swindoll

Grace is not something outside of you. In fact, your very desire for grace is due to grace that is already working in you. . . . Grace is the Self. It is not something to be acquired. All that is necessary is to know its existence.

Ramana Maharshi

Grace strikes us when we are in great pain and restlessness. It strikes us when we walk through the dark valley of a meaningless and empty life.

Paul Tillich

Grace is not a strange, magic substance which is subtly filtered into our souls to act as a kind of spiritual penicillin. Grace is unity, oneness within ourselves, oneness with God.

Thomas Merton

If my life attests to nothing else, it's that I've done absolutely nothing to merit God's grace and favor. . . . It was a gift.

Bill McCartney

Spiritual grace originates from the divine Ground of all being, and it is given for the purpose of helping man to achieve his final end, which is to return out of time and selfhood to that Ground.

Aldous Huxley

GOD

Of all the definitions of God, none is indeed so well put as the Biblical statement I AM THAT I AM.

Ramana Maharshi

God is love. And in every moment of genuine love we are dwelling in God and God in us.

Paul Tillich

God is the expression of the intelligent universe.

Kahlil Gibran

God is as present as the air.

Michael Hollings

The Infinite Goodness has such wide arms that it takes whatever turns to it.

Dante Alighieri

St. Francis ordered a plot to be set aside for the cultivation of flowers when the convent garden was made, in order that all who saw them might remember the Eternal Sweetness.

Thomas of Celano

God = He . . . She . . . it . . . It . . . I.

Peter Russell

22

If God is male, not female, then men are intrinsically better than women. It follows then, that until the emphasis on maleness in the image of God is redressed, the women of the world cannot be entirely liberated. For if God is thought of as simply and exclusively male, then the very cosmos seems sexist.

Paul Moore

If oxen and horses . . . could paint . . . , horses would paint the forms of the gods like horses, and oxen like oxen. . . .

Xenophanes

The biggest problem I face while teaching Sunday school is convincing the preschoolers that Barney is not God.

Robert G. Lee

The Lord can be addressed by any name that tastes sweet to your tongue, or pictured in any form that appeals to your sense of wonder and awe.

Satya Sai Baba

Shall I say: Creator, Sustainer, Pardoner, Near One, Distant One, Incomprehensible One, God both of flowers and stars, God of the gentle wind and of terrible battles, Wisdom, Power, Loyalty and Truthfulness, Eternity and Infinity, you the All-Merciful, you the Just One, you Love itself?

Karl Rahner

In the beginning was the Word and the Word was sound.

Don G. Campbell

Behold! A sacred voice is calling you! All over the
sky a sacred voice is calling you!

Black Elk

God is the Being . . . that may properly only be
addressed, not expressed.

Martin Buber

God is our name for the last generalization to
which we can arrive.

Ralph Waldo Emerson

Be still and know that I am God.

The Bible

The blessings of Wakan Tanka flowed over the Indian like rain showered from the sky. Wakan Tanka was not aloof, apart, and ever seeking to quell evil forces. He did not punish the animals and the birds, and likewise He did not punish man. . . . For there was never a question as to the supremacy of an evil power over and above the power of Good. There was but one ruling power, and that was *Good.*

Chief Luther Standing Bear

If you say that God is good, great, blessed, wise or any such thing, the starting point is this: God is.

Bernard of Clairvaux

God . . . is a verb. . . .

R. Buckminster Fuller

26

I have never understood why it should be considered derogatory to the Creator to suppose that He has a sense of humor.

William Ralph Inge

The world is proof that God is a committee.

Bob Stokes

Even bein' Gawd ain't no bed of roses.

Marc Connelly

God don't make no mistakes. That's how he got to be God.

Archie Bunker

I cannot imagine a God who rewards and punishes the objects of His own creation, whose purposes are modeled after our own—a God, in short, who is a reflection of human frailty.

Albert Einstein

I cannot say I believe. I know! I have had the experience of being gripped by something that is stronger than myself, something that people call God.

Carl Jung

It is difficult to know why God reveals Himself to some and plays the game of hide-and-seek with others.

Papa Ramdas

God created man in his own image, says the Bible; philosophers reverse the process: they create God in theirs.

Georg Christoph Lichtenberg

If God is your target, you're in luck, because *God is so big, you can't miss.*

Neale Donald Walsch

We could not seek God unless He were seeking us.

Thomas Merton

God speaks chiefly through dreams and visions.

Carl Jung

I am convinced that the universe is under the control of a loving purpose, and that in the struggle for righteousness man has cosmic companionship. Behind the harsh appearance of the world there is a benign power.

Martin Luther King, Jr.

He's not a "safe" or a "tame" God, securely lodged behind the bars of a distant heaven; he has the most annoying manner of showing up when we least want him; of confronting us in the strangest ways.

Robert McAfee Brown

To ask for a proof of the existence of God is on a par with asking for a proof of the existence of beauty.

Walter T. Stace

God is dead. . . .

Friedrich Wilhelm Nietzsche

What can you say about a society that says that God is dead and Elvis is alive?

Irv Kupcinet

30

Whoever it was who searched the heavens with a telescope and found no God would not have found the human mind if he had searched the brain with a microscope.

George Santayana

My atheism, like that of Spinoza, is true piety towards the universe and denies only gods fashioned by men in their own image, to be servants of their human interests.

George Santayana

I have never been afflicted by the idea of God. I have never awakened in the middle of the night and said, without the idea of God my life would be meaningless.

Clifton Fadiman

To you I'm an atheist. To god I'm the loyal opposition.

Woody Allen

31

The atheists have produced a Christmas play. It's called *Coincidence on 34th Street.*

Jay Leno

In spite of all the yearnings of men, no one can produce a single fact or reason to support the belief in God and in personal immortality.

Clarence Darrow

An atheist is a man who watches a Notre Dame-Southern Methodist University football game and doesn't care who wins.

Dwight D. Eisenhower

The best reply to an atheist is to give him a good dinner and ask him if he believes there is a cook.

Louis Nizer

There are no atheists in foxholes.

William T. Cummings

Selfishness is the only real atheism.

Israel Zangwill

How can I believe in God when just last week I got my tongue caught in the roller of an electric typewriter.

Woody Allen

I'd hate to be an atheist, die, and meet God only to have him say, "I'm sorry, but I don't believe in you."

Robert G. Lee

It does me no injury for my neighbor to say there are twenty gods or no God. It neither picks my pocket nor breaks my leg.

Thomas Jefferson

I gave in, and admitted that God was God.

C.S. Lewis

If someone were to ask me whether I believed in God, or saw God, or had a particular relationship with God, I would reply that I don't separate God from my world in my thinking. I feel that God is everywhere.

Robert Fulghum

We turn to Spirit for help when our foundations are shaking, only to find out that it is Spirit who is shaking them.

Dan Millman

What you are is God's gift to you; what you make of it is your gift to God.

Anthony Dalla Villa

The only God worth talking about is a God that cannot be talked about.

Walter Kaufmann

I fear God, yet am not afraid of him.

Thomas Browne

God depends on us. It is through us that God is achieved.

André Gide

God is never pushy when taking hold
of a man's heart.

Bill McCartney

Suppose a man in hiding and he stirs, he shows his
whereabouts thereby; and God does the same. No one could
ever have found God; he gave himself away.

Meister Eckhart

I am the Alpha and Omega, the beginning and the
end, the first and the last.

The Bible

FAITH

Faith dares the soul to go farther than it can see.

William Clark

One doesn't discover new lands without consenting to lose sight of the shore for a very long time.

André Gide

Faith is knowing there is an ocean because you have seen a brook.

William Arthur Ward

Faith is so rare—and religion so common—because no one wants to live between first base and second base. Faith is the in-between space where you're not sure you'll make it to second base. You've let go of one thing and haven't yet latched onto another. Most of us choose the security of first base.

Richard Rohr

No ray of sunlight is ever lost, but the green which it wakes into existence needs time to sprout, and it is not always granted to the sower to live to see the harvest. All work that is worth anything is done in faith.

Albert Schweitzer

Faith is better understood as a verb than a noun, as a process than a possession. It is an on-again, off-again rather than once-and-for-all. Faith is not sure where you're going but going anyway.

Frederick Buechner

38

If you gain, you gain all; if you lose, you lose nothing. Wager, then, without hesitation, that He exists.

Blaise Pascal

Doubt is part of all religion. All the religious thinkers were doubters.

Isaac Bashevis Singer

A faith which does not doubt is a dead faith.

Miguel de Unamuno y Jugo

In the days of captivity, chained to a wall, I found myself asking God in a silent shout, "Why? Why me!"

Lawrence Martin Jenco, O.S.M.

Doubt is not the opposite of faith; it is one element of faith.

Paul Tillich

There are two ways to slide easily through life: to believe everything or to doubt everything; both ways save us from thinking.

Alfred Korzybski

He who has no faith in himself can never have faith in God.

Vivekananda

The rose window high above seems black and formless. But when we enter, and see it backlit by the sun, it dazzles in astonishing splendor. And it reminds us that without faith, we too are but stained-glass windows in the dark.

George Bush

Faith is the bird that sings when the dawn
is still dark.

Rabindranath Tagore

Faith supplies staying power. . . . Anyone can keep
going when the going is good, but some extra ingredient is
needed to keep you fighting when it seems that everything is
against you.

Norman V. Peale

I do not pretend to see light, but I do see gleams,
and I know I am right to follow those gleams.

Agnellus Andrew, S.D.C.

Faith is a gift of the spirit that allows the soul to
remain attached to its own unfolding.

Thomas Moore

Live in simple faith . . .
Just as this
Trusting cherry
Flowers, fades, and falls.

Issa

It is the heart which experiences God, and not
the reason. This, then, is faith: God felt by the heart,
not by the reason.

Blaise Pascal

Treat the other man's faith gently; it is all he has to
believe with. His mind was created for his own thoughts, not
yours or mine.

Henry S. Haskins

It is as absurd to argue men, as to torture them,
into believing.

John Henry Newman

All I have seen teaches me to trust the Creator for all I have not seen.

Ralph Waldo Emerson

Faith is nothing more than the conscious choice of the God within.

Mohandas K. Gandhi

Imagine walking into a darkened room. We put our hands in front of us, afraid we are going to bump into a piece of furniture or slip on a rug. We walk very slowly. This is very much what God calls us to on the journey of faith.

Richard Rohr

In these matters the only certainty is that there is nothing certain.

Pliny the Elder

43

PROBLEMS

There is no such thing as a problem without a gift for you in its hands. You seek problems because you need their gifts.

Richard Bach

In the Buddhist tradition, difficulties are considered to be so important to a life of growth and peace that a Tibetan prayer actually asks for them. . . . It is felt that when life is too easy, there are fewer opportunities for genuine growth.

Richard Carlson

Man is the only kind of varmint sets his own trap, baits it, then steps in it.

John Steinbeck

Here is my lesson from the heavy rain: on your way, you meet a shower. You dislike to get wet, so you hurry along the streets running under the eaves. Still, you get wet all the same. As long as you accept that you will get wet, you won't suffer from being wet.

Minoru Tanaka

The worst thing in your life may contain seeds of the best. When you see crises as an opportunity, your life becomes not easy, but more satisfying.

Joe Kogel

Bless a thing and it will bless you. Curse it and it will curse you. . . . If you bless a situation, it has no power to hurt you, and even if it is troublesome for a time, it will gradually fade out, if you sincerely bless it.

Emmet Fox

Blame someone else and get on with your life.

Alan Woods

45

The best years of your life are the ones in which you decide your problems are your own. You don't blame them on your mother, the ecology or the President. You realize that you control your own destiny.

Albert Ellis

That some good can be derived from every event is a better proposition than that everything happens for the best, which assuredly it does not.

James K. Feibleman

Not everything that is more difficult is more meritorious.

Thomas Aquinas

No problem is so big or so complicated that it can't be run away from.

Charles Schulz

46

Never bear more than one kind of trouble at a time. Some people bear all three—all they have had, all they have now, and all they expect to have.

Edward Everett Hale

One way to get high blood pressure is to go mountain climbing over molehills.

Earl Wilson

Storms make oaks take deeper root.

George Herbert

The lowest ebb is the turn of the tide.

Henry Wadsworth Longfellow

It sometimes happens that, if the water is too clear, then the fish will no longer dwell there.

Minoru Tanaka

I dreamt last night oh marvelous air
That honeybees were in my heart making honey
    out of my old failures.

Antonio Machado

A little boy was asked how he learned to skate. "Oh, by getting up every time I fell down," he answered.

David Seabury

Don't have a cow, man.

Bart Simpson

ACTION

The question is: Who will get to heaven first—the man who talks or the man who acts?

Melvin B. Tolson

When a man surrenders himself as a slave to the Divine Lord he realizes at the end that all his actions are the actions of God. He loses his mind-ness. This is what is meant by "doing the will of God."

Paul Brunton

Do not be too squeamish about your actions. All life is an experiment.

Ralph Waldo Emerson

49

Nothing would be done at all if we waited until we could do it so well that no one could find fault with it.

John Henry Newman

Do what you can where you are with what you've got.

Theodore Roosevelt

Fasting is good for the soul, but works of love are better.

Tom Crouch

I am often praying for others when I should be doing things for them. It's so much easier to pray for a bore than to go and see him.

C.S. Lewis

We ought to do good to others as simply and naturally as a horse runs, or a bee makes honey, or a vine bears grapes season after season without thinking of the grapes it has borne.

Marcus Aurelius

You can't cross the sea merely by staring at the water.

Rabindranath Tagore

The only way to get positive feelings about yourself is to take positive actions. Man does not live as he thinks, he thinks as he lives.

Vaughan Quinn, O.M.I.

We must alter our lives in order to alter our hearts, for it is impossible to live one way and pray another.

William Law

The truth of the matter is that you always know the right thing to do. The hard part is doing it.

H. Norman Schwarzkopf

The road to holiness necessarily passes through the world of action.

Dag Hammarskjöld

No matter what we feel or know, no matter what our potential gifts or talents, only action brings them to life. Many of us understand concepts such as commitment, courage, and love, but we truly know only when we do.

Dan Millman

WISDOM

Real wisdom is the ability to take God's truth and apply it to life. All it requires is a heart for God and some plain old common sense.

Tony Evans

Wisdom is not communicable. The wisdom which a wise man tries to communicate always sounds foolish. Knowledge can be communicated, but not wisdom. One can find it, live it, be fortified by it, do wonders through it, but one cannot communicate and teach it.

Hermann Hesse

Wisdom does not attain completeness except through the living of life.

Rabindranath Tagore

Not to know certain things is a great part of wisdom.

Hugo Grotius

It is not wise to be wiser than necessary.

Philippe Quinault

Everything should be made as simple as possible but not simpler.

Albert Einstein

The first key to wisdom is constant and frequent questioning, for by doubting we are led to question and by questioning we arrive at truth.

Peter Abelard

The older I grow the more I distrust the familiar doctrine that age brings wisdom.

H.L. Mencken

As a solid rock is not shaken by the wind, wise people falter not amidst blame and praise.

Dhammapada

What wisdom can you find that is greater than kindness?

Jean Jacques Rousseau

55

It requires wisdom to understand wisdom; the music is nothing if the audience is deaf.

Walter Lippmann

Wisdom is the reward you get for a lifetime of listening when you'd have preferred to talk.

Doug Larson

All wisdom can be stated in two lines: What is done for you—allow it to be done. What you must do yourself— make sure you do it.

Khawwas

Wisdom consists not as much in knowing what to do in the ultimate as in knowing what to do next.

Herbert Hoover

Wisdom is to see the miraculous in the common.

Ralph Waldo Emerson

Be careful to get out of an experience all the wisdom that is in it—not like the cat that sits down on a hot stove. She will never sit down on a hot stove lid again—and that is well; but also she will never sit down on a cold one anymore.

Mark Twain

No one can give you wisdom. You must discover it for yourself on the journey through life, which no one can take for you.

Sun Bear

The sage must distinguish between knowledge and wisdom. Knowledge is of things, acts and relations. . . . To become one with God is the only wisdom.

The Upanishads

EGO

It is only by forgetting yourself that you draw near to God.

Henry David Thoreau

Make your ego porous.

Rainer Maria Rilke

Ego is to the true self what a flashlight is to a spotlight.

John Bradshaw

The problem is that ego can convert anything to its own use, even spirituality. Ego is constantly attempting to acquire and apply the teachings of spirituality for its own benefit.

Chögyam Trungpa

The ego follows us like a dark shadow. Its power is intoxicating and addicting but ultimately destructive.

Deepak Chopra

Self-importance is our greatest enemy. Think about it—what weakens us is feeling offended by the deeds and misdeeds of our fellowmen. Our self-importance requires that we spend most of our lives offended by someone.

Carlos Castaneda

I myself do nothing. The Holy Spirit accomplishes all through me.

William Blake

That man attains peace who, abandoning all desires, moves about without the attachment and longing, without the sense of "I" and "mine."

The Bhagavad-Gita

Who told you that you were permitted to settle in? Who told you that this or that would last forever? Did no one ever tell you that you will never feel at home in the world?

Stanislaw Baranczak

Don't give me so much credit for my work. The credit is not all mine. I mean only that I am merely the instrument through which a Supreme Intelligence carries on His work.

Thomas Edison

Become a passage, a hollow flute, and divine songs will flow through you.

Thomas Moore

The music of this opera [Madame Butterfly] was dictated to me by God; I was merely instrumental in putting it on paper and communicating it to the public.

Giacomo Puccini

The game is not about becoming somebody, it's about becoming nobody.

Baba Ram Dass

Ego is not a four-letter word.

Don Steele

What's wrong with this egotism? If a man doesn't delight in himself and the force in him and feel that he and it are wonders, how is all life to become important to him?

Sherwood Anderson

To hold on to power, you must guard against self-inflation or ego-tripping. Constantly envision yourself as servant, not proprietor, of the powers around us all. Honor their mystery. And let them use you.

Malidoma Somé

Attachments to things, identifications with things, keep alive a thousand useless "I"s in a man. These "I"s must die in order that the big I may be born.

G.I. Gurdjieff

The seed that is to grow must lose itself as a seed; and they that creep may graduate through chrysalis to wings. Wilt thou, O mortal, cling to husks which falsely seem to you the self?

Wu Ming Fu

ONENESS

The moment a person realizes his oneness with the Infinite Spirit, he recognizes himself as a spiritual being, and no longer a physical, material being.

Ralph W. Trine

Joy is the realization of the truth of oneness, the oneness of our soul with the world and of the world-soul with the supreme lover.

Rabindranath Tagore

Nothing less than becoming one with the universe will suffice.

Morihei Ueshiba

All know that the drop merges into the ocean but few know that the ocean merges into the drop.

Kabir

It was a morning in early summer. A silver haze shimmered and trembled over the lime trees. The air was laden with their fragrance. The temperature was like a caress. I remember—I need not recall—that I climbed up a tree stump and felt suddenly immersed in Itness. I did not call it by that name. I had no need for words. It and I were one.

Bernard Berenson

You are both individual and one with all that is.

Gary Zukav

There are no others.

Ramana Maharshi

We are all connected to everyone and everything in the universe. Therefore, everything one does as an individual affects the whole. All thoughts, words, images, prayers, blessings, and deeds are listened to by all that is.

Serge Kahili King

When we try to pick out anything by itself, we find it hitched to everything in the universe.

John Muir

To the analytical mind, the universe is broken apart. It is split into the known and unknown, into the seen and unseen. But, in the mystic contemplation, all things are seen as one.

Abraham Joshua Heschel

We sit together, the mountain and I, until only the mountain remains.

Li Po

This we know: All things are connected
like the blood which unites one family.
All things are connected.
Whatever befalls the earth
befalls the sons of the earth.
Man did not weave the web of life.
He is merely a strand on it.
Whatever he does to the web
He does to himself.

Chief Seattle

The philosophical implication of quantum mechanics
is that all the things in our universe (including us) that appear
to exist independently are actually part of one all-encompassing
organic pattern, and that no parts of that pattern are ever really
separate from it or from each other.

Fritjof Capra

All life is one; therefore, there cannot be God and man, nor a universe and God. A god not in the world is a false god, and a world not in God is unreal. All things return to one, and one operates in all.

Nyogen Senzaki

The great heresy and the only heresy is the idea that anything is separate, distinct, and different essentially from other things. That is a wandering from natural fact and law, for nature is nothing if not coordination, cooperation, mutual helpfulness; and the rule of fundamental unity is perfectly universal: everything in the universe lives for everything else.

G. de Purucker

We do not exist separate from each other, we do not exist separate from the environment that we live in. We are all one. That separateness that you perceive just does not objectively exist: it is not there.

A.H. Almaas

It is a terrible, an inexorable law that one cannot deny the humanity of another without diminishing one's own: in the face of one's victim, one sees oneself.

James Baldwin

Peace. . . comes within the souls of men when they realize their relationship, their oneness, with the universe and all its powers, and when they realize that at the center of the Universe dwells Wakan Tanka, and that this center is really everywhere, it is within each of us.

Black Elk

We live as ripples of energy in the vast ocean of energy.

Deepak Chopra

A fella ain't got a soul of his own, but on'y a piece of a big one.

John Steinbeck

DUALITY

The sense of duality vanishes completely once you realize your identity with God. You and He become one. The drop becomes one with the ocean.

Papa Ramdas

Nothing is born, nothing is destroyed. Away with your dualism, your likes and dislikes. Every single thing is just One Mind.

Huang Po

The physical universe was created when Oneness became duality, and we can see this duality, this yin and yang, everywhere in the universe, in every atom, every action, and in every function of the human body. Yin and yang are manifest everywhere, except at the very center of being, the perfect point of balance, at that infinite moment when the future becomes the past.

Robert Tisserand

Thus, the wise man is able to give himself gracefully to seemingly contradictory experiences, because he knows that they belong to different seasons of life, all of which are necessary to the whole. Spring and winter, growth and decay, creativity and fallowness, health and sickness, power and impotence, and life and death all belong within the economy of being.

Sam Keen

Yin and yang, male and female, strong and weak, rigid and tender, heaven and earth, light and darkness, thunder and lightning, cold and warmth, good and evil. . . . the interplay of opposite principles constitutes the universe.

Confucius

People who have not been in Narnia sometimes think that a thing cannot be good and terrible at the same time.

C.S. Lewis

Good is that which makes for unity; Evil is that which makes for separateness.

Aldous Huxley

Y̲ou yourself are participating in the evil, or you are not alive. Whatever you do is evil for somebody. This is one of the ironies of the whole creation.

Joseph Campbell

E̲vil = unfinished creation.

Ted Black

I̲t is one of the great troubles of life that we cannot have any unmixed emotions. There is always something in our enemy that we like, and something in our sweetheart that we dislike.

William Butler Yeats

T̲hey live in freedom who have gone beyond the dualities of life. Competing with no one, they are alike in success and failure and content with whatever comes to them.

The Bhagavad-Gita

When you make the two one, and when you make the inside like the outside and the outside like the inside, and the above like the below, and when you make the male and the female one and the same . . . then you will enter [the Kingdom].

Gnostic Gospel of Thomas

Whenever you say, "This is beautiful," you have brought ugliness into the world. Don't you see. Whenever you say, "I love," you have brought hatred into the world. Whenever you say, "You are my friend," you have brought enmity into the world. Whenever you say, "This is good, right, moral," you have brought immorality into the world, you have brought the devil into the world. In deep silence, when you don't know what is good and what is bad, you don't utter any labels and names, in that silence the duality disappears. The world becomes one.

Osho

God's mind perceives all sin and evil in the idea of the corresponding good, not in the form of sin; for instance, he knows lying in the idea of truth.

Meister Eckhart

The conflict of forces and the struggle of opposing wills are of the essence of our universe and alone hold it together.

Havelock Ellis

We live on the brink of disaster because we do not know how to let life alone. We do not respect the living and fruitful contradictions and paradoxes of which true life is full.

Thomas Merton

The test of first-rate intelligence is the ability to hold two opposed ideas in the mind at the same time, and still retain the ability to function.

F. Scott Fitzgerald

In seeking truth you have got to get both sides of a story.

Walter Cronkite

It was the best of times, it was the worst of times; it was the age of wisdom, it was the age of foolishness; it was the epoch of belief, it was the epoch of incredulity; it was the season of light, it was the season of darkness; it was the spring of hope, it was the winter of despair.

Charles Dickens

The rose and the thorn, and sorrow and gladness are linked together.

Moslih Eddin Saadi

The maker fused duality in all; sorrow and joy the foremost of all these pairs.

Manu

The opposite of a correct statement is a false statement; but the opposite of a profound truth may be another profound truth.

Niels Bohr

Beyond the pairs of opposites of which the world consists, other, new insights begin.

Hermann Hesse

We die, and we do not die.

Shunryu Suzuki

If you think my King is beautiful, you should see His Queen.

Uranda

One gets glimpses, even in our country, of that which is ageless—heavy thought in the face of an infant, and frolic childhood in that of a very old man.

C.S. Lewis

In the Buddhist approach, life and death are seen as one whole, where death is the beginning of another chapter of life. Death is a mirror in which the entire meaning of life is reflected.

Sogyal Rinpoche

The night was made for Love and Rest and Peace—a time when new things might begin and germinate and grow until they are ready to come forth into the Light; for there are things of God that cannot live in the Light of God until they have first been caused to grow in the darkness of God.

Uranda

In the midst of winter, I finally learned that there was in me an invincible summer.

Thomas Carlyle

To confront a person with his own shadow is to show him his own light.

Carl Jung

Most men have a dual interpretation of themselves—two pictures of their two selves in separate rooms. In one room are hung all the portraits of their virtues, done in bright, splashing, glorious colors, but with no shadows and no balance. In the other room hangs the canvas of self-condemnation. Instead of keeping these two pictures isolated from one another, we must look at them together and blend them into one.

Joshua Loth Liebman

No healing can take place until we decide to think actively about the dark side.

Robert Bly

You are your own friend and you are your own enemy.

The Bhagavad-Gita

The key word is paradox. As a fool I sidestep the either/or choices of logic and choose both.

Ken Feit

We are destined to evolve beyond the nature of duality.

Gary Zukav

A vital aspect of the enlightened state is the experience of an all-pervading unity. "This" and "that" no longer are separate entities. They are different forms of the same thing. . . . Everything is a manifestation of that which is. That which is, is.

Gary Zukav

80

CREATION

W hat does God do all day long? God lies in a maternity bed giving birth.

Meister Eckhart

W hat really interests me is whether God had any choice in the creation of the world.

Albert Einstein

T he event of creation did not take place so many kalpas or aeons ago, astronomically or biologically speaking. Creation is taking place every moment of our lives.

D.T. Suzuki

Man unites himself with the world in the process of creation.

Erich Fromm

God made us, not because He knew what we would do, but to find out what we would do.

Damon Knight

God is really only another artist. He invented the elephant, the giraffe and the cat. He has no real style. He just goes on trying other things.

Pablo Picasso

No somber God could have made a bullfrog or a giraffe.

George A. Buttrick

For time itself is contained in the universe, and therefore when we speak about creation we should not inquire at what time it happened.

Thomas Aquinas

The human spirit lives on creativity and dies in conformity and routine.

Vilayat Inayat Khan

It may be that our role on this planet is not to worship God, but to create him.

Arthur C. Clark

In order to create there must be a dynamic force, and what force is more potent than love?

Igor Stravinsky

The creation of the world is not only a process which moves from God to humanity. God demands newness from humanity; God awaits the works of human freedom.

Nicolas Berdyaev

The deepest experience of the creator is feminine, for it is the experience of receiving and bearing.

Rainer Maria Rilke

We have no reason to suppose that we are the Creator's last word.

George Bernard Shaw

God sure thunk up some stuff.

John Preston Downs

In the beginning was the Thing. And one thing led to another.

Tom Robbins

God is not finished. His highest divine attribute is His creativeness and that which is creative exists always in the beginning stage. God is eternally in Genesis.

Isaac Bashevis Singer

Why assume so glibly that the God who presumably created the universe is still running it? It is certainly conceivable that He may have finished it and then turned it over to lesser gods to operate.

H.L. Mencken

A baby is God's opinion that the world should go on.

Carl Sandburg

MUSIC

Music is the basis of the whole creation.
In reality the whole of creation is music, and what we call
music is simply a miniature of the original music, which is
creation itself, expressed in tone and rhythm.

Hazrat Inayat Khan

In the beginning was noise. And noise begat rhythm.
And rhythm begat everything else.

Mickey Hart

The human being is essentially sound, vibrations,
and melody. . . .

Holger Kalweit

What song did the great fireball sing? What tune accompanied the formation of the galaxies? The music that ushered in the cosmos played on, inside us and around us.

Brian Swimme

The Indians long ago knew that music was going on permanently and that hearing it was like looking out a window at a landscape which didn't stop when one turned away.

John Cage

The drum is sacred. Its round form represents the whole universe, and its steady beat is the pulse, the heart, throbbing at the center of the universe.

Nick Black Elk

I saw the music!

David Tame

God invented rock 'n' roll so kids could hear him.

"Mac" Malloy

I dance not to get better nor to fix myself, I dance to remember that I am not sick.

Malidoma Somé

Music washes away from the soul the dust of everyday life.

Berthold Auerbach

In music's sweet harmony, I have all the proof I need of God.

Pat Conroy

LIFE

It's all about letting life live you, not you living life.

Ralph Mitchell

We must be willing to get rid of the life we've planned, so as to have the life that is awaiting us. . . . The old skin has to be shed before the new one is to come.

Joseph Campbell

Courage is almost a contradiction in terms. It means a strong desire to live taking the form of a readiness to die.

G.K. Chesterton

Life don't run away from nobody. Life runs at people.

Joe Frazier

There is a strange reluctance on the part of most people to admit that they enjoy life.

William Lyon Phelps

My grandfather always said that living is like licking honey off a thorn.

Louis Adamic

Once we truly know that life is difficult—once we truly understand and accept it—then life is no longer difficult. Because once it is accepted, the fact that life is difficult no longer matters.

M. Scott Peck

When I hear somebody sigh, "Life is hard," I am always tempted to ask, "Compared to what?"

Sydney Harris

The man with the clear head is the man who . . . looks life in the face, realizes that everything in it is problematic, and feels himself lost. And this is the simple truth: that to live is to feel oneself lost.

José Ortega y Gasset

Many years ago a very wise man named Bernard Baruch took me aside and put his arm around my shoulder. "Harpo my boy," he said, "I'm going to give you three pieces of advice, three things you should always remember." My heart jumped and I glowed with expectation. I was going to hear the magic password to a rich, full life from the master himself. "Yes sir?" I said. And he told me the three things. I regret that I've forgotten what they were.

Harpo Marx

Let life be a deep let-go. See God opening millions of flowers every day without forcing the buds.

Osho

Living at risk is jumping off the cliff and building your wings on the way down.

Ray Bradbury

Were the diver to think of the jaws of the shark he would never lay hands on the precious pearl.

Sa'di

From nowhere we came; into nowhere we go. What is life? It is the flash of a firefly in the night. It is the breath of a buffalo in the wintertime. It is the shadow which runs across the grass and loses itself in the sunset.

Crowfoot

Life is no brief candle to me. It is a sort of splendid torch which I have got hold of for the moment, and I want to make it burn as brightly as possible before handing it on to future generations.

George Bernard Shaw

Life's most persistent and urgent question is: What are you doing for others?

Martin Luther King, Jr.

If you miss love, you miss life.

Leo Buscaglia

Life is what happens while you are making other plans.

John Lennon

Life is suffering.

Buddha

Life's a tough proposition, and the first hundred years are the hardest.

Wilson Mizner

Just when I found out the meaning of life, they changed it.

George Carlin

If you can spend a perfectly useless afternoon in a perfectly useless manner, you have learned how to live.

Lin Yutang

Our life is frittered away by detail . . . simplify, simplify.

Henry David Thoreau

Showing up is eighty percent of life.

Woody Allen

One of the greatest things you have in life is that nobody has the authority to tell you what you want to be.

Jaime Escalante

Many men die at twenty-five and aren't buried until they are seventy-five.

Benjamin Franklin

When we are really honest with ourselves we must admit our lives are all that really belong to us. So it is how we use our lives that determines the kind of men we are.

César Chávez

I want to be able to say in the last four seconds of my life that I tried to do my best. Only then will I smile. Only then will I be at peace with myself.

Rubén Blades

My life is my message.

Mohandas K. Gandhi

They lived and laughed and loved and left.

James Joyce

HAPPINESS

The summit of happiness is reached when a person is ready to be what he is.

Erasmus

Nearly all mankind is more or less unhappy because nearly all do not know the true Self. Real happiness abides in Self-knowledge alone. All else is fleeting. To know one's Self is to be blissful always.

Ramana Maharshi

Happiness is a form of courage.

Holbrook Jackson

Happiness is experienced when your life gives you what you are willing to accept.

Ken Keyes

Happiness makes up in height for what it lacks in length.

Robert Frost

When a little bubble of joy appears in your sea of consciousness, take hold of it and keep expanding it. Meditate on it and it will grow larger. Keep puffing at the bubble until it breaks its confining walls and becomes a sea of joy.

Paramahansa Yogananda

Love of life is the fundamental ingredient of all recipes for happiness. . . .

Robert Muller

Remember that happiness is as contagious as gloom. It should be the first duty of those who are happy to let others know of their gladness.

Maurice Maeterlinck

One of the sanest, surest, and most generous joys of life comes from being happy over the good fortune of others.

Archibald Rutledge

About ninety percent of the things in our lives are right and about ten percent are wrong. If we want to be happy, all we have to do is to concentrate on the ninety percent that are right and ignore the ten percent that are wrong.

Dale Carnegie

Anyone who is happy all the time is nuts.

Leo Rosten

The search for happiness is one of the chief sources of unhappiness.

Eric Hoffer

It is pretty hard to tell what does bring happiness; poverty and wealth have both failed.

Kin Hubbard

A man is happy so long as he chooses to be happy.

Aleksandr Solzhenitsyn

I don't sing because I'm happy; I'm happy because I sing.

William James

Spiritual inebriation is this: that a man receives more sensible joy and sweetness than his heart can either contain or desire. Spiritual inebriation brings forth many strange gestures in men. It makes some sing and praise God because of their fullness of joy, and some weep with great tears because of their sweetness of heart. It makes one restless in all his limbs, so that he must run and jump and dance; and so excites another that he must gesticulate and clap his hands.

John of Ruysbroeck

My life has no purpose, no direction, no aim, no meaning, and yet I'm happy. I can't figure it out. What am I doing right?

Charles Schulz

Happy people plan actions, they don't plan results.

Dennis Wholey

There are a great many people in our society who are happy, but since they don't know they're happy, they're not happy.

Theodore Isaac Rubin

Most men pursue pleasure with such breathless haste that they hurry past it.

Sören Kierkegaard

The wisest of the men I've talked to mostly have said the same things: talk to your father and mother, talk to your wife, talk to your kids. Give your kids a safe place to grow, be there for the small moments, appreciate yourself, don't be afraid to be too happy.

Bill Scanlon

One of the things I keep learning is that the secret of being happy is doing things for other people.

Dick Gregory

I am more and more convinced that our happiness or unhappiness depends more on the way we meet the events of life than on the nature of those events themselves.

Alexander Humboldt

The truth is, there's no better time to be happy than right now. If not now, when? Your life will always be filled with challenges. It's best to admit this to yourself and decide to be happy anyway.

Richard Carlson

Don't worry. Be happy.

Bobby McFerrin

103

THE PRESENT

Be here now.

Ram Dass

May you live all the days of your life.

Jonathan Swift

The time is now, the place is here. Stay in the present. You can do nothing to change the past, and the future will never come exactly as you plan or hope for.

Dan Millman

To live with God is to live always in the present, with him who is the eternal Now.

John A.T. Robinson

I expect to pass through this world but once. Any good therefore that I can do, or any kindness or abilities that I can show to any fellow creature, let me do it now. Let me not defer or neglect it, for I shall not pass this way again.

William Penn

The present time has one advantage over every other—it is our own.

Charles Colton

There's a sign in a casino in Las Vegas that reads, "You must be present to win."

Jack Kornfield

Only in a hut built for the moment can one live without fear.

Kamo No Chomei

I've developed a new philosophy—I only dread one day at a time.

Charles Schulz

One of the most tragic things I know about human nature is that all of us tend to put off living. We are all dreaming of some magical rose garden over the horizon—instead of enjoying the roses that are blooming outside our windows today.

Dale Carnegie

Life is now in session. Are you present?

B. Copeland

We are not particularly concerned with the past, because our connection with the truth is always in the present; nor are we greatly concerned with the future, because our connection with the truth is always in the present.

Martin Exeter

There is only one courage and that is the courage to go on dying to the past, not to collect it, not to accumulate it, not to cling to it. We all cling to the past, and because we cling to the past we become unavailable to the present.

Osho

Nothing today need conform to anything of yesterday.

Jesse Jennings

God delights to isolate us every day and hide from us the past and the future. . . .

Ralph Waldo Emerson

The present moment. . . . has several dimensions. . . . the present of things past, the present of things present, and the present of things future. . . .

Augustine

I have an existential map. It has "You are here" written all over it.

Steven Wright

The future is much like the present, only longer.

Dan Quisenberry

I shall tell you a great secret, my friend. Do not wait for the last judgment. It takes place every day.

Albert Camus

To a large degree, the measure of our peace of mind is determined by how much we are able to live in the present moment.

Richard Carlson

This—the immediate, everyday, and present experience—is IT, the entire and ultimate point for the existence of the universe.

Alan Watts

109

I know absolutely nothing. That is why each new day, each new moment, is truly an adventure.

Ross Fields

God speaks to all individuals through what happens to them moment by moment.

Jean Pierre de Caussade

The other day a man asked me what I thought was the best time of life. "Why," I answered, "now."

David Grayson

FOREVER

Surely God would not have created such a being as man, with an ability to grasp the infinite, to exist only for a day! No, man was made for immortality.

Abraham Lincoln

Neither experience nor science has given man the idea of immortality. . . . The idea of immortality rises from the very depths of his soul—he feels, he sees, he knows that he is immortal.

François Guizot

I have
Immortal longings in me.

William Shakespeare

It is eternity now. I am in the midst of it. It is about me in the sunshine; I am in it, as the butterfly in the light-laden air. Nothing has to come, it is now. Now is eternity, now is immortal life.

Richard Jeffries

Either the soul is immortal and we shall not die, or it perishes with the flesh and we shall not know that we are dead. Live, then, as if you were immortal.

André Maurois

I don't want to achieve immortality through my work. I want to achieve it through not dying.

Woody Allen

112

I want to live forever. If you carry the love we shared to others, I will live for a long, long time.

John Guarnaschelli

Every aspect of yourself is immortal, even the parts you judge most harshly.

Deepak Chopra

Eternity is not the hereafter. Eternity has nothing to do with time. . . . This is it. If you don't get it here, you won't get it anywhere. The experience of eternity right here and now is the function of life. Heaven is not the place to have the experience; here's the place to have the experience.

Joseph Campbell

LOVE

Love is all. Without Love there is nothing, in Love is all that is Eternal. Love includes all and is all.

Uranda

I believe that the reason for life is for each of us simply to grow in love. I believe that this growth in love will contribute more than any other force to establish the Kingdom of God on earth.

Leo Tolstoy

Everything has to do with loving and not loving.

Rumi

Someday after mastering the winds, the waves, the tides and gravity, we shall harness for God the energies of Love, and then, for the second time in the history of the world, man will discover fire.

Pierre Teilhard de Chardin

Love is not something we do, love is something we are.

Cliff Barry

Love is letting-be. . . .

John Macquarrie

Love is the only way to grasp another human being in the innermost core of his personality.

Victor Frankl

The first duty of love is to listen.

Paul Tillich

To love is the most important thing in life. But what do we mean by love? When you love someone because that person loves you in return surely that is not love. To love is to have that extraordinary feeling of affection without asking anything in return.

Krishnamurti

Love is the ability and willingness to allow those that you care for to be what they choose for themselves without any insistence that they satisfy you.

Wayne Dyer

There is no difficulty that enough love will not conquer; no disease that enough love will not heal; no door that enough love will not open.

Emmet Fox

All problems boil down to limited choices, and the choice we often forget is love.

Tom Daly

Love is the only force capable of transforming an enemy into a friend.

Martin Luther King, Jr.

I know no one in any time who has succeeded in loving every man he met.

Martin Buber

If you love one person more than another this is not true love; it is an attachment created by desire. To love all things equally. . . . is true love.

Saradamma

The purest love lies where it is least expected—in unattachment.

Deepak Chopra

You cannot unconditionally love someone. You can only be unconditional love. . . .You don't love another, you are another.

Stephen Levine

Nobody out there can love you the way you want to be loved. Only you can do that.

John-Roger

Our first duty is not to hate ourselves.

Vivekananda

Every part of our personality that we do not love will become hostile to us.

Robert Bly

People who do not experience self-love have little or no capacity to love others.

Nathaniel Branden

The arrogance of reason has separated us from love.

Kabir

Our present economic, social and international arrangements are based, in large measure, upon organized lovelessness.

Aldous Huxley

Passionate hatred can give meaning and purpose to an empty life.

Eric Hoffer

The price of hating other human beings is loving oneself less.

Eldridge Cleaver

120

I have decided to stick with love. Hate is too great a burden to bear.

Martin Luther King, Jr.

The best way to know God is to love many things.

Vincent Van Gogh

All love is Divine. Let it never be said that physical or romantic love is less than God's Love, for ideas cannot be apart from their source.

Alan Cohen

Infantile love follows the principle: I love because I am loved. Mature love follows the principle: I am loved because I love.

Eric Fromm

Part of living with love is also learning how to say "no." This may sound selfish, but in fact what it means is that we are choosing how we will love the world that day.

Bernie Siegel

There are never enough "I love you's."

Lenny Bruce

To the degree that you truly love, you find it easy to ignore the things that would be condemned and judged, both in yourself and others.

Uranda

The really precious moments of a man's life seem to be spaced in accordance with his own openness for loving.

Ron Kearns

Love is something you can leave behind you when you die. It's that powerful.

John Lame Deer

When we come to the last moment of this lifetime, and we look back across it, the only thing that's going to matter is "What was the quality of our love?"

Richard Bach

It is possible that a man can be so changed by love as hardly to be recognized as the same person.

Terence

SUFFERING

Out of suffering have emerged the strongest souls.

Edwin Chapin

Love your suffering. Do not resist it, do not flee from it. Give yourself to it.

Hermann Hesse

The more the diamond is cut, the brighter it sparkles; and what seems hard dealing, there God has no end in view but to perfect His people.

Thomas Guthrie

Suffering turns the mind towards God.
Suffering infuses mercy in the heart and softens it.
Suffering strengthens.

Sivananda

Truly, it is in the darkness that one finds the light, so when we are in sorrow, then this light is nearest of all to us.

Meister Eckhart

Tell your heart that the fear of suffering is worse than the suffering itself.

Paulo Coelho

I have been through some terrible things in my life, some of which actually happened.

Mark Twain

As I've gotten older, I find I am able to be nourished more by sorrow and to distinguish it from depression.

Robert Bly

If you see suffering all around you, it is just a reflection of your own inner suffering. If you want to alleviate suffering, go to the root cause which is the suffering inside yourself.

Annamalai Swami

Suffering is a journey which has an end.

Matthew Fox

We have no right to ask when a sorrow comes, "Why did this happen to me?" unless we ask the same question for every joy that comes our way.

Philip Bernstein

Let us teach ourselves and our children the necessity for suffering and the value thereof, the need to face problems directly and to experience the pain involved.

M. Scott Peck

Much of your pain is self-chosen. It is the bitter potion by which the physician within you heals your sick self.

Kahlil Gibran

Everything hurts.

Michaelangelo Antonioni

Letting go of our suffering is the hardest work we will ever do.

Stephen Levine

Human pain does not let go of its grip at one point in time. Rather, it works its way out of our consciousness over time. There is a season of sadness. A season of anger. A season of tranquility. A season of hope.

Robert Veninga

When someone suffers, and it is not you, he comes first. His very suffering gives him priority. . . . To watch over a man who grieves is a more urgent duty than to think of God.

Elie Wiesel

While grief is fresh, every attempt to divert it only irritates.

Samuel Johnson

The deep pain that is felt at the death of every friendly soul arises from the feeling that there is in every individual something which is inexpressible, peculiar to him alone, and is, therefore, absolutely and irretrievably lost.

Arthur Schopenhauer

No one ever told me that grief felt so like fear. I am not afraid, but the sensation is like being afraid. The same fluttering in the stomach, the same restlessness, the yawning. I keep on swallowing.

C.S. Lewis

I spent a lot of time crying in our home. I don't mean sobbing, I mean truly crying, as hard as a human being possibly can do it. I got up every day and hoped I'd make it through to the next. By two o'clock every day, I was exhausted. Grief does that.

Farland Bottoms

Jesus wept.

The Bible

God will not look you over for medals, degrees or diplomas, but for scars.

Elbert Hubbard

PRAYER

Prayer is the contemplation of the facts of life from the highest point of view.

Ralph Waldo Emerson

Prayer is our humble answer to the inconceivable surprise of living.

Abraham Joshua Heschel

When we pray to God we must be seeking nothing—nothing.

Francis of Assisi

A simple prayer for the soul's journey is: "I will to will Thy will." Such a simple form of prayer is proper, it seems, on almost any occasion.

Ralph Blum

Prayer is not the moment when God and humans are in relationship, for that is always. Prayer is taking initiative to intentionally respond to God's presence.

L. Robert Keck

To wish to pray is a prayer in itself.

Georges Bernanos

Prayer takes place in the heart, not in the head.

Carlo Carretto

Prayer, we like to hope, is a moment of true speaking. At that instant we become the words we say. There is no deception, no ego to defend, no manufactured self.

Barry Holtz

I pray by breathing.

Thomas Merton

The great thing is to pray, even if it be in vague and inarticulate fashion.

John Strutt

Most people when they pray, talk to God rather than with Him. They don't take time to listen, in deep inner silence, for His answer.

J. Donald Walters

In the foothills of the Himalayas. . . . one hears the prayer: "Oh Lord, we know not what is good for us. Thou knowest what it is. For it we pray."

Harry Fosdick

God is not a cosmic bell-boy for whom we can press a button to get things.

Harry Fosdick

Father expected a good deal of God. He didn't actually accuse God of inefficiency, but when he prayed, his tone was loud and angry, like that of a dissatisfied guest in a carefully managed hotel.

Clarence Day

The object of most prayers is to wangle an advance on good intentions.

Robert Brault

Whatever a man prays for, he prays for a miracle. Every prayer reduces itself to this: "Great God, grant that twice two be not four."

Ivan Turgenev

Personal prayer, it seems to me, is one of the simplest necessities of life, as basic to the individual as sunshine, food and water—and at times, of course, more so. By prayer I believe we mean an effort to get in touch with the Infinite . . . prayer multiplies the strength of the individual and brings within the scope of his capabilities almost any conceivable objective.

Dwight D. Eisenhower

In the life of the Indian there is only one inevitable duty—the duty of prayer—the daily recognition of the Unseen and Eternal.

Ohiyesa

Prayer gives a man the opportunity of getting to know a gentleman he hardly ever meets. I do not mean his maker, but himself.

Dean W.R. Inge

Prayer is not a stratagem for occasional use, a refuge to resort to now and then. It is rather like an established residence for the innermost self. All things have a home: the bird has a nest, the fox has a hole, the bee has a hive. A soul without prayer is a soul without a home.

Abraham Joshua Heschel

Don't pray when it rains if you don't pray when the sun shines.

Satchel Paige

Yank some groans out of your prayers and shove in some shouts.

Billy Sunday

Ask God's Spirit to give you the kind of hunger that will produce change.

Randy Phillips

Meditation is one of the few things in life that is not about DOING but about BEING.

Rick Fields

The notes I handle no better than many pianists. But the pauses between the notes—ah, that is where the art resides.

Artur Schnabel

When someone says, "Oh, I can worship God anywhere," the answer is, "Do you?"

James Pike

The quieter you become the more you can hear.

Baba Ram Dass

Happy is the man who has learned the secret
of coming to God daily in prayer. Fifteen minutes alone with
God every morning before you start the day can change
circumstances and remove mountains.

Billy Graham

If you do not pray, everything can disappoint you by
going wrong. If you do pray, everything can still go wrong,
but not in a way that will disappoint you.

Hubert van Zeller

I never went to bed in my life and I never ate a meal
in my life without saying a prayer. I know my prayers have
been answered thousands of times, and I know that I never
said a prayer in my life without something good coming of it.

Jack Dempsey

SOUL

No one can give a definition of the soul. But we know what it feels like. The soul is the sense of something higher than ourselves, something that stirs in us thoughts, hopes, and aspirations which go out to the world of goodness, truth and beauty. The soul is a burning desire to breathe in this world of light and never to lose it—to remain children of light.

Albert Schweitzer

Other words long associated with the word soul amplify it further: mind, spirit, heart, life, warmth, humanness, personality, individuality, intentionality, essence, innermost, purpose, emotion, quality, virtue, morality, sin, wisdom, death, God.

James Hillman

The soul is partly in eternity and partly in time.

Marsilio Ficino

Just as unconditional love is one of the manifestations of soul growth, there are other attributes as well: forgiveness, courage, patience, faith, compassion, generosity, wisdom. An evolved soul requires all of these qualities, in proper balance.

John Gray

"Soul" is found in the quality of what I am doing. . . . "nourishing the soul" means making sure I attend to those things that give my life richness and depth of meaning.

Robert Fulghum

We're souls having a human experience.

Brian Weiss

By soul I mean, first of all, a perspective rather than a substance, a viewpoint toward things rather than a thing itself.

James Hillman

We all experience "soul moments" in life—when we see a magnificent sunrise, hear the call of the loon, see the wrinkles in our mother's hands, or smell the sweetness of a baby. During these moments, our body, as well as our brain, resonates as we experience the glory of being a human being.

Marion Woodman

Feeling is the language of the Soul.

Neale Donald Walsch

Some people tell me I'd invented the sounds they call soul—but I can't take any credit. . . . Soul is just the way black folk sing when they leave themselves alone.

Ray Charles

As we think, act, and express ourselves in accord with the way the soul would have us think, act, and express ourselves, we learn to sound the OM. We grow spiritually.

Carl Japikse

It is with the soul that we grasp the essence of another human being, not with the mind, nor even with the heart.

Henry Miller

To the soul, there is hardly anything more healing than friendship.

Thomas Moore

Soul is our appetite, driving us to eat from the banquet of life. People filled with the hunger of soul take food from every dish before them, whether it be sweet or bitter.

Matthew Fox

142

Every soul is the hostage of its own deeds.

The Koran

Man's supreme and final battles are to be fought out in his own soul.

Abraham Aaron Neuman

The great malady of the twentieth century, implicated in all of our troubles and affecting us individually and socially, is "loss of the soul." When soul is neglected, it doesn't just go away; it appears symptomatically in obsessions, addictions, violence, and loss of meaning. Our temptation is to isolate these symptoms or to try to eradicate them one by one; but the root problem is that we have lost our wisdom about the soul, even our interest in it.

Thomas Moore

You know the disease in Central Africa called sleeping sickness. . . . There also exists a sleeping sickness of the soul. Its most dangerous aspect is that one is unaware of its coming. That is why you have to be careful. As soon as you notice the slightest sign of indifference, the moment you become aware of the loss of a certain seriousness, of longing, of enthusiasm and zest, take it as a warning. You should realize your soul suffers if you live superficially.

Albert Schweitzer

We make soul with our behavior, for soul doesn't come already made in heaven. It is only imaged there, an unfulfilled project trying to grow down.

James Hillman

When the soul wishes to experience something, she throws an image of the experience out before her and enters into her own image.

Meister Eckhart

The soul needs an intense, full-bodied spiritual life as much as and in the same way that the body needs food.

Thomas Moore

Your soul is that part of you that is immortal.

Gary Zukav

The soul is not like God: she is identical with Him

Meister Eckhart

We inherit from our ancestors gifts so often taken for granted. . . . Each of us contains within our fragile vessels of skin and bones and cells this inheritance of soul. We are links between the ages, containing past and present expectations, sacred memories and future promise.

Edward Sellner

First, soul refers to the deepening of events into experiences; second, the significance soul makes possible, whether in love or in religious concern, derives from its special relation with death. And third, by soul I mean the imaginative possibility in our natures, the experiencing through reflective speculation, dream, image, and fantasy—that mode which recognizes all realities as primarily symbolic or metaphorical.

James Hillman

I think that love is given us so that we can see a soul. And this soul we see is the highest conception of excellence and truth we can bring forth: This soul is our reflected self. And from seeing what one soul is, we imagine what all souls may be . . . and thus we reach God, who is the Universal Soul.

Elbert Hubbard

We see the world piece by piece, as the sun, the moon, the animal, the tree; but the whole, of which these are the shining parts, is the soul.

Ralph Waldo Emerson

146

TRUTH

Truth is the highest thing that man may keep.

Geoffrey Chaucer

I never did give anybody hell. I just told the truth and they thought it was hell.

Harry S. Truman

God offers to every mind its choice between truth and repose.

Ralph Waldo Emerson

Man can live his truth, his deepest truth, but cannot speak it.

Archibald MacLeish

The truth knocks on the door and you say, "Go away, I'm looking for the truth," and so it goes away. Puzzling.

Robert Persig

Believe those who are seeking the truth; doubt those who find it.

André Gide

If you would know the truth, hear out the heretics as well as the believers.

Leonard Roy Frank

148

If you tell the truth you don't have to
remember anything.

Mark Twain

One of the most untruthful things possible . . . is a
collection of facts, because they can be made to appear so
many different ways.

Karl Meninger

That's not a lie; it's a terminological inexactitude.

Alexander Haig

Sometimes you have to look reality in the eye
and deny it.

Garrison Keillor

149

"Hello," he lied.

Don Carpenter

The liar's punishment is not in the least that he is not believed, but that he cannot believe anyone else.

George Bernard Shaw

Truth hurts—not the searching after; the running from.

John Eyberg

It is inner abandonment that leads men to the highest truth.

Henry Suso

150

S ay not, "I have found the truth" but rather, "I have found a truth."

Kahlil Gibran

W hen truth is discovered by someone else, it loses something of its attractiveness.

Aleksandr Solzhenitsyn

T o truly find God, truth needs to be found independently from the opinions of others. The truth has to be found in our hearts; it has to be totally personal, totally in our inner aloneness.

A.H. Almaas

N ever, ever, regret or apologize for believing that, when one man or one woman decides to risk addressing the world with truth, the world may stop what it is doing and hear.

Robert Fulghum

151

Our own life is the instrument with which we experiment with Truth.

Thich Nhat Hanh

The color of truth is gray.

André Gide

It does not require many words to speak the truth.

Chief Joseph

GRATITUDE

Thank you, God. I'm not sure why. But thank you.

Juan Ramón Jiménez

A thankful person is thankful under all circumstances.
A complaining soul complains even if he lives in paradise.

Baha'u'llah

Say alleluia always, no matter the time of day, no
matter the season of life.

Benedict of Nursia

Gratitude is not only a virtue, it also is part of a practical philosophy of daily life. There is no wiser way of living than to remember every morning what Life has given us, and to lift up our thought in thankfulness for every bounty we possess.

Ernest Holmes

There are two kinds of gratitude . . . the sudden kind we feel for what we take, the larger kind we feel for what we give.

Edward Arlington Robinson

You can't be depressed and grateful at the same time.

Randall Miller

Feeling gratitude and not expressing it is like wrapping a present and not giving it.

William Arthur Ward

In ordinary life we hardly realize that we receive a great deal more than we give, and that it is only with gratitude that life becomes rich.

Dietrich Bonhoeffer

I feel a very unusual sensation—if it is not indigestion, I think it must be gratitude.

Benjamin Disraeli

Isn't God good to me?

Louis B. Mayer

When you arise in the morning, give thanks for the morning light, for your life and strength. Give thanks for your food and the joy of living.

Tecumseh

i thank You God for most this amazing
day for the leaping greenly spirits of trees
and a blue true dream of sky, and for everything
which is natural which is infinite which is yes

e.e. cummings

If the only prayer you say in your whole life is
"thank you," that would suffice.

Meister Eckhart

COMPASSION

Great compassion is the root of all forms of worship.

Dalai Lama

Compassion is . . . a spirituality and a way of living and walking through life. It is the way we treat all there is in life—ourselves, our bodies, our imaginations and dreams, our neighbors, our enemies. . . . Compassion is a spirituality as if creation mattered. It is treating all creation as holy and as divine . . . which is what it is.

Matthew Fox

Compassion means to lay a bridge over to the other without knowing whether he wants to be reached.

Henri J.M. Nouwen

I never ask the wounded person how he feels; I myself become the wounded person.

Walt Whitman

Compassion is the basis of all truthful relationship: it means being present with love—for ourselves and for all life, including animals, fish, birds, and trees.

Ram Dass

It is through compassion that a person achieves the highest peak and deepest reach in his or her search for self-fulfillment.

Arthur Jersild

Without an awareness of our feelings we cannot experience compassion. How can we share the sufferings and the joys of others if we cannot experience our own?

Gary Zukav

Compassion for myself is the most powerful healer of them all.

Theodore Isaac Rubin

How far you go in life depends on your being tender with the young, compassionate with the aged, sympathetic with the striving, and tolerant of the weak and strong. Because someday in life you will have been all of these.

George Washington Carver

Never hesitate to hold out your hand; never hesitate to accept the outstretched hand of another.

Pope John XXIII

A sure way for someone to lift himself up is by helping to lift someone else.

Booker T. Washington

Every human being has the potential for compassion. I have chosen to pay more attention to it.

Dalai Lama

To me compassion provides a setting in which essential change can occur, and it provides protection so that this can happen without unnecessary damage.

Michael Cecil

Compassion simply stated is leaving other people alone. . . . You are available to another human being, to provide what they need, to the extent that they ask.

Ram Dass

Tell me how much you know of the sufferings of your fellow men and I will tell you how much you have loved them.

Helmut Thielicke

O Great Spirit, help me never judge another until I have walked two weeks in his moccasins.

Edwin Laughing Fox

The whole idea of compassion is based on a keen awareness of the interdependence of all these living beings, which are all part of one another and all involved in one another.

Thomas Merton

DEATH

What the caterpillar calls a tragedy, the Master calls a butterfly.

Richard Bach

What better can the Lord do for a man than take him home when he has done his work?

Charles Kingsley

Life is a great surprise, I do not see why death should not be a greater one.

Vladimir Nabokov

Let children walk with Nature, let them see the beautiful blendings and communions of death and life, their joyous inseparable unity, as taught in woods and meadows . . . and they will learn that death is stingless indeed, and as beautiful as life.

John Muir

There is no death. Only a change of worlds.

Chief Seattle

Nothing is dead. People feign themselves dead, and endure mock funerals and mournful obituaries. And there they stand, looking out the window, sound and well in some strange new disguise.

Ralph Waldo Emerson

Science has found that nothing can disappear without a trace. Nature does not know extinction. All it knows is transformation.

Wernher von Braun

He who pretends to look on death without fear lies. All men are afraid of dying; this is the great law of sentient beings, without which the entire human species would soon be destroyed.

Jean-Jacques Rousseau

Death holds terror for us. This is because we think we are merely physical bodies subject to birth, growth, decay and death. To shed this fear we must realize that we are immortal and that even if the body perishes we are not going to perish.

Papa Ramdas

When your time comes to die, be not like those whose hearts are filled with the fear of death, so when their time comes they weep and pray for a little more time to live their lives over again in a different way. Sing your death song, and die like a hero going home.

Tecumseh

Are you afraid you don't know how to die? Don't worry. Nature will take care of that for you.

Marco Vasso

Man lives freely only by his readiness to die.

Mohandas K. Gandhi

A solemn funeral is inconceivable to the Chinese mind.

Lin Yutang

My grandfather had a wonderful funeral. My grandfather was a very insignificant man, actually. At his funeral his hearse followed the other cars. It was a nice funeral, though, you would have liked it—it was a catered funeral. It was held in a big hall with accordion players. On the buffet table there was a replica of the deceased in potato salad.

Woody Allen

I can't die. I'm booked.

George Burns

Between projects I go into the park and bite the grass and wail, "Why do You make me aware of the fact that I have to die one day?" God says, "Please, I have Chinese people yelling at me, I haven't time for this." I say all right.

Mel Brooks

166

It's not that I'm afraid to die. I just don't want to be there when it happens.

Woody Allen

I shall hear in heaven.

Ludwig von Beethoven

The late F.W.H. Myers used to tell how he asked a man at a dinner table what he thought would happen to him when he died. The man tried to ignore the question, but, on being pressed, replied: "Oh well, I suppose I shall inherit eternal bliss, but I wish you wouldn't talk about such unpleasant subjects."

Bertrand Russell

Everybody has got to die but I've always believed an exception would be made in my case. Now what?

William Saroyan

A man's dying is more the survivor's affair than his own.

Thomas Mann

Never say about anything, "I have lost it," but only "I have given it back." Is your child dead? It has been given back. Is your wife dead? She has been returned.

Epictetus

The first piercing grief eventually becomes a kind of ever-present sorrow that doesn't seem to want to go away ever, but then it does; or, rather, it grows into something else, something you know you can live with, although at the same time you know you'll never forget.

Chuck Norris

Each departed friend is a magnet that attracts us to the next world.

Jean Paul Richter

168

Nothing hurts more than the deep fear that deceased sons and daughters are being forgotten because no one ever talks of them again.

Ronald Knapp

Whom the Gods love dies young.

Meander

There is no suicide for which all society is not responsible.

Cyril Connolly

Death ends a life. But it doesn't end a relationship.

Hal Holbrook

It is the duty of the doctor to prolong life. It is not his duty to prolong death.

Thomas Horder

A dying man needs to die as a sleeping man needs to sleep, and there comes a time when it is wrong, as well as useless, to resist.

Stewart Alsop

No really great song can ever attain full purport till long after the death of its singer—till it has accrued and incorporated the many passions, many joys and sorrows, it has itself aroused.

Walt Whitman

Día de Los Muertos [Day of the Dead] . . . reminds us that those loved ones who have gone before us can be as close as a plate of hot food, a can of cold beer or the flash of a bright memory.

Lalo Lopez

170

From what we are told by most of those who have reported such [near-death] incidents, the moment of death can be one of unparalleled beauty, peace and comfort—a feeling of total love and total acceptance. This is possible even for those involved in horrible accidents in which they suffered very serious injuries.

Kenneth Ring

I noted that the faces of people who have a terminal disease, and who have come to terms with their own impending death, have a look that is a marvelous combination of tranquility and incredible power and insight.

Mal Warshaw

When are you going to die? In fifty years, twenty, ten, five, today? Last time I checked, no one had told me. . . . The truth is, none of us has any idea how long we have to live.

Richard Carlson

All my life, in every place, every day, in every light and color, asleep and awake, happy and sad, poor and rich, I have felt death by my side. I'm beginning to think that she likes having me as a living friend.

Juan Ramón Jiménez

The realization of certain death ought to be renewed every morning.

Minoru Tanaka

Death is not the enemy of life, but its friend, for it is the knowledge that our years are limited which makes them so precious.

Joshua Loth Liebman

Seeing death as the end of life is like seeing the horizon as the end of the ocean.

David Searls

If a person offend you, and you are in doubt as to whether it was intentional or not, do not resort to extreme measures; simply watch your chance and hit him with a brick.

Mark Twain

Some people advise me to forgive and forget. They do not realize that this is almost impossible. Jesus, the wounded healer, asks us to forgive, but he does not ask us to forget. . . . I don't believe that forgetting is one of the signs of forgiveness. I forgive, but I remember. I do not forget the pain, the loneliness, the ache, the terrible injustice. But I do not remember it to inflict guilt or some future retribution.

Lawrence Martin Jenco, O.S.M.

Forgiveness is the fragrance of the violet that clings to the heel that crushed it.

George Roemisch

MIRACLES

Be realistic. Plan for a miracle.

Osho

The most astonishing thing about miracles is that they happen.

G.K. Chesterton

Miracles do not happen in contradiction to nature, but only in contradiction to that which is known to us of nature.

Augustine

We have been looking for the burning bush, the parting of the sea, the bellowing voice from heaven. Instead we should be looking at the ordinary day-by-day events in our lives for evidence of the miraculous.

M. Scott Peck

Everything is miraculous. It is a miracle that one does not melt in one's bath.

Pablo Picasso

Why, who makes much of a miracle?
As to me I know nothing else but miracles—
To me every hour of night and day is a miracle,
Every cubic inch of space a miracle.

Walt Whitman

The oddest miracle is that we perceive so few miracles.

Brian Knave

Complacency in the presence of miracles is like opening the door to your own tomb.

Rod Steiger

I have learned to use the word impossible with the greatest caution.

Wernher von Braun

The most important tool the artist fashions through constant practice is faith in his ability to produce miracles when they are needed.

Mark Rothko

The highest part of the art of life is the expectation of miracles.

William Bolitho

NATURE

I believe in God, only I spell it Nature.

Frank Lloyd Wright

N ature's intent is neither food, nor drink, nor clothing, nor comfort, nor anything else in which God is left out. . . . secretly nature seeks, hunts, tries to ferret out the track on which God may be found.

Meister Eckhart

N ature is the living, visible garment of God.

Goethe

The universe is the primary revelation of the divine, the primary scripture, the primary focus of divine-human communion.

Thomas Berry

My father considered a walk among the mountains as the equivalent of church-going.

Aldous Huxley

Nature is too thin a screen; the glory of the omnipresent God bursts through everywhere.

Ralph Waldo Emerson

The natural world is a spiritual house. . . . Man walks there through forests of physical things that are also spiritual things, that watch him with affectionate looks.

Charles Baudelaire

Every single creature is full of God and is a book about God.

Meister Eckhart

What is man without the beasts? If all the beasts were gone, men would die from great loneliness of spirit, for whatever happens to the beasts also happens to man. All things are connected. Whatever befalls the earth befalls the sons of the earth.

Chief Seattle

Animals are not brethren, they are not underlings, they are other nations, caught up with ourselves in the net of life and time, fellow prisoners of the splendor and travail of the earth.

Henry Boston

I really don't think I could consent to go to Heaven if I thought there were to be no animals there.

George Bernard Shaw

Nowadays we don't think much of a man's love for an animal; we laugh at people who are attached to cats. But if we stop loving animals, aren't we bound to stop loving humans too?

Aleksandr Solzhenitsyn

He who sustains God's creatures is as though he had created them.

Tanhuma

Every part of this earth is sacred to my people. Every shining pine needle, every sandy shore, every mist in the dark woods, every clearing and [every] humming insect is holy in the memory and experience of my people.

Chief Seattle

Won't you come into the garden? I would like my roses to see you.

Richard Sheridan

Everything is blooming most recklessly; if it were voices instead of colors, there would be an unbelievable shrieking into the heart of the night.

Rainer Maria Rilke

The flowers of the earth do not grudge at one another, though one be more beautiful and fuller of virtue than another; but they stand kindly one by another, and enjoy one another's virtue.

Jakob Boehme

Flowers always make people better, happier and more helpful; they are sunshine, food and medicine to the soul.

Luther Burbank

Gardening is an active participation in the deepest mysteries of the universe.

Thomas Berry

It's difficult to think anything but pleasant thoughts while eating a home-grown tomato.

Lewis Grizzard

Every blade of grass has its angel that bends over it and whispers, "Grow, grow."

The Talmud

I never knew how soothing trees are—many trees and patches of open sunlight, and tree presences; it is almost like having another being.

D.H. Lawrence

As the poet said, "Only God can make a tree." Probably because it's so hard to get the bark on.

Woody Allen

The sun, with all those planets revolving around it and dependent upon it, can still ripen a bunch of grapes as if it had nothing else in the universe to do.

Galileo Galilei

I have seen the sea when it is stormy and wild; when it is quiet and serene; when it is dark and moody. And in all its moods, I see myself.

Martin Buxbaum

I have a seashell collection; maybe you've seen it? I keep it on beaches all over the world.

Stephen Wright

Nature is our mother. Because we live cut off from her, we get sick.

Thich Nhat Hanh

The Creator created the Earth, our Mother Earth, and gave her many duties, among them the duty to care for us, His people. He put things upon Mother Earth for the benefit of all. And as we travel around today we see that our Mother Earth is still doing her duty, and for that we are very grateful. So let us put our minds together as one and give thanks. And let it be that way. . . .

Irving Powless, Sr.

The old Lakota was wise. He knew that man's heart away from nature becomes hard; he knew that lack of respect for growing, living things soon led to lack of respect for humans too.

Chief Luther Standing Bear

As the human species awakens itself as a collection of immortal souls learning together, care for the environment and the earth will become a matter of the heart, the natural response of souls moving towards their full potential.

Gary Zukav

192

If the Earth is indeed our body and blood, then in destroying it we are committing a slow and gruesome suicide.

Ken Wilber

Hills are always more beautiful than stone buildings, you know. Living in a city is an artificial existence. Lots of people hardly ever feel real soil under their feet, see plants grow except in flower pots, or get far enough beyond the street light to catch the enchantment of a night sky studded with stars. When people live far from scenes of the Great Spirit's making, it's easy for them to forget his laws.

Tatanga Mani

To learn to see, to learn to hear, you must do this— go into the wilderness alone.

Don José Matsuwa

Adopt the pace of nature. Her secret is patience.

Ralph Waldo Emerson

Do not be afraid to suffer; give the heaviness back to the weight of the earth; mountains are heavy, seas are heavy.

Rainer Maria Rilke

When despair for the world grows in me and I wake in the night at the least sound in fear of what my life and my children's lives may be, I go and lie down where the wood drake rests in his beauty on the water, and the great heron feeds. I come into the peace of wild things who do not tax their lives with forethought of grief. I come into the presence of still water. And I feel above me the day-blind stars waiting with their light. For a time I rest in the grace of the world and am free.

Wendell Berry

Unknowingly, we plow the dust of stars, blown about us by the wind, and drink the universe in a glass of rain.

Ihab Hassan

Our bodies are . . . communities in relationship with the earth. Our bodily fluids carry the same chemicals as the primeval seas. . . . Our bones contain the sugar that once flowed in the sap of now-fossilized trees. The nitrogen which binds our bones together is the same as that which binds nitrates to the soil.

James Nelson

The earth and myself are of one mind.

Chief Joseph

Never does nature say one thing and wisdom another.

Juvenal

Science is not only compatible with spirituality; it is a profound source of spirituality.

Carl Sagan

A physicist is just an atom's way of looking at itself.

Niels Bohr

What I know of the divine science and Holy Scripture I learnt in woods and fields.

Bernard of Clairvaux

What person has ever come near to nature and not seen therein the revelation of God's spirit? Through all the physical universe there runs the all-pervading life of God—hence is every particle of this universe in itself a revelation of God.

John Haynes Holmes

The God who is in fire, who is in water, who has entered into the whole world, who is in plants, who is in trees—to that God be adoration!

The Upanishads

BODY

Good men spiritualize their bodies.

Benjamin Whichcote

The body is the instrument of the soul.

Gary Zukav

Body and soul are not two substances but one. They are man becoming aware of himself in two different ways.

C.F. von Weizsacker

Our body is our most sacred resource available to experience the soul. . . . For example, when I wander from my soul path, my body signals me with strong physical messages, such as headaches, illness or fatigue.

Benjamin Shield

Man has no Body distinct from his Soul; for that called Body is a portion of Soul discerned by the five Senses, the chief inlets of Soul.

William Blake

My great religion is a belief in the blood, the flesh, as being wiser than the intellect. We can go wrong in our minds. But what our blood feels and believes and says is always true.

D.H. Lawrence

There is nothing the body suffers that the soul does not profit by.

George Meredith

The people who live in fear of disease are the people who get it. Anxiety quickly demoralizes the whole body and lays it open to the entrance of disease.

James Allen

Do not neglect this body. This is the house of God; take care of it. Only in this body can God be realized.

Nisargadatta

I have visited in my wanderings shrines and other places of pilgrimage. But I have not seen another shrine like my own body.

Saraha

The body is a tabernacle in which the transmissable human spirit is carried for a while, a shell for the immortal seed that dwells in it and has created it.

George Santayana

The body is the soul's house. Shouldn't we therefore take care of our house so that it doesn't fall into ruin?

Philo Judaeus

Often the wisdom of the body clarifies the despair of the spirit.

Marion Woodman

If you want to find the answers to the Big Questions about your soul, you'd best begin with the Little Answers about your body.

George Sheehan

Our own physical body possesses a wisdom which we who inhabit the body lack. We give it orders which make no sense.

Henry Miller

200